Mastiff as Pets

A Complete Mastiff Owner's Guide

Mastiff Dogs General Info, Purchasing, Care, Cost, Diet, Health, Supplies, Grooming, Training and More Included!

By Lolly Brown

Copyrights and Trademarks

All rights reserved. No part of this book may be reproduced or transformed in any form or by any means, graphic, electronic, or mechanical, including photocopying, recording, taping, or by any information storage retrieval system, without the written permission of the author.

This publication is Copyright ©2019 NRB Publishing, an imprint. Nevada. All products, graphics, publications, software and services mentioned and recommended in this publication are protected by trademarks. In such instance, all trademarks & copyright belong to the respective owners. For information consult www.NRBpublishing.com

Disclaimer and Legal Notice

This product is not legal, medical, or accounting advice and should not be interpreted in that manner. You need to do your own due-diligence to determine if the content of this product is right for you. While every attempt has been made to verify the information shared in this publication, neither the author, neither publisher, nor the affiliates assume any responsibility for errors, omissions or contrary interpretation of the subject matter herein. Any perceived slights to any specific person(s) or organization(s) are purely unintentional.

We have no control over the nature, content and availability of the web sites listed in this book. The inclusion of any web site links does not necessarily imply a recommendation or endorse the views expressed within them. We take no responsibility for, and will not be liable for, the websites being temporarily unavailable or being removed from the internet.

The accuracy and completeness of information provided herein and opinions stated herein are not guaranteed or warranted to produce any particular results, and the advice and strategies, contained herein may not be suitable for every individual. Neither the author nor the publisher shall be liable for any loss incurred as a consequence of the use and application, directly or indirectly, of any information presented in this work. This publication is designed to provide information in regard to the subject matter covered.

Neither the author nor the publisher assume any responsibility for any errors or omissions, nor do they represent or warrant that the ideas, information, actions, plans, suggestions contained in this book is in all cases accurate. It is the reader's responsibility to find advice before putting anything written in this book into practice. The information in this book is not intended to serve as legal, medical, or accounting advice.

Foreword

Mastiffs are large dog breeds that are known to be gentle giants. They are very clever and docile by nature, and they love nothing more than to be at home, and involved with everyone and everything. They form very strong bonds with their keepers, which means that these dogs thrive on human connection, and as such are best with families where at least one person stays at home even if everyone else is out of the house. Mastiff dogs are also known as "English Mastiff" and because of their sheer size, they need a spacious environment to roam around in both indoors and outdoors so that they can feel a sense of freedom.

Mastiffs, like any other dog breeds, need to be given physical and mental stimulation through various forms of exercise and playtime. This will keep them healthy and they won't put on weight which can make them prone to obesity and other healthy issues. Mastiff dogs however may not be the best choice for first – time dog keepers because they need to be handled and trained at an early age so that when they mature they will be well – mannered pets.

These dogs are incredibly strong and can easily pull their owners so you need to be quite firm on them and already have prior experience to keeping large dogs.

Table of Contents

Mastiff Dogs: A Large Breed with the Heart of a Lion 1

Chapter One: Mastiff Physique and Temperament 2

    The English Mastiff Official Breed Standard 3

    Temperament 5

Chapter Two: Mastiff as Pets 8

    Mastiff as Household Pets 9

        Are they a good choice for first time owners? 9

        What about prey drive? 9

        What about playfulness? 10

        What about adaptability? 10

        What about separation anxiety? 11

        What about excessive barking? 11

        Do Mastiffs like water? 11

        Are Mastiffs good watchdogs? 12

    Trainability 13

        Reinforcement Training 14

        Handling Aggression 16

    Children and Other Pets 18

    Pros and Cons 20

        Positives 20

        Negatives 20

Chapter Three: Caring for a Mastiff 22

Caring for a Mastiff Puppy 23

Things you'll need for your puppy 24

Keeping the noise down... 25

Keeping vet appointments... 26

What about older Mastiffs when they reach their senior years? 26

Exercise... 29

Average Cost to Keep and Care for a Mastiff 31

Knowing How a Dog was Bred 32

Dogs and Children... 34

Feeding... 36

Feeding Guide for a Mastiff Puppy 38

Feeding guide for an adult Mastiff..................................... 40

Grooming... 40

Chapter Four: Mastiff Buying Advice...................................... 42

Before You Buy 43

Other Factors to Consider.. 44

Chapter Five: Mastiff Health and Caring Tips 50

Common Health Issues of Mastiffs....................................... 51

What about spaying and neutering?.................................... 53

What about obesity problems?... 53

What about allergies? 54

Participating in health schemes 55

What about breed specific breeding restrictions? 55

What about Assured Breeder Requirements? 55

Testing For Hip Dysplasia in Dogs 56

What is hip dysplasia? 57

Testing for Hip Dysplasia 58

Mastiff Dog Hereditary Health and Health Testing 60

Other Health Issues 64

Chapter Six: Breeding Mastiff 66

Gestation Period Calendar 67

Getting Ready For Birth 74

The First Stages of Labor 80

What Happens Once Labor is in Full Swing 84

Chapter Seven: Mastiff Breed Rating 88

Mastiff Breed Rating 89

Intelligence 99

Glossary of Dog Terms 102

Index 108

Photo Credits 112

References 113

Mastiff Dogs: A Large Breed with the Heart of a Lion

"What the lion is to a cat, the Mastiff is to a dog"

Mastiffs are among the earliest dog breeds in the world but obviously, the breeds we now see are not exactly the same as those mastiffs that were seen centuries ago. There are records of the breed that date back to the 15th century. Back then, these dogs were used to protect and guard people, along with other similar – looking dogs.

Mastiff Dogs: A Large Breed with the Heart of a Lion

What's fascinating is that the actual origins of the Mastiff breed still remain a mystery. With this said, it is thought that these large dogs originally came from Asia, and that it was the Phoenician traders who introduce the breed to other parts of the world. When the Romans arrived in the shores of England, they were so amazed by the Mastiff dogs and because of that, they took them back to Rome.

The Normans were also impressed by the Mastiff breed they discovered on their own when they conquered the British Isles. In fact, there were records of this dog breed having been bought by Gauls and took it with them into battle. As such, it's quite fair to say that large mastiff dog breeds have been around for two thousand years or so. When the Romans left England, people began using this canine as watch dogs on their farms and over their livestock. They were known as Tied Dogs or Bandogs even if they were used as watch dogs. Mastiff dogs proved to be great hunting dogs although there was a law in Norman that decreed that dog breeds should have three toes cut off from their front feet in order to stop them from killing or chasing the King's deer.

Another great history about the Mastiff breed is one that involves a Knight named Piers Leigh who was mortally wounded after fighting the French army. It was said that his mastiff dogs guarded him in order to prevent anyone from approaching. The mastiff turned out to be a female, and it was from her lineage that the famous Lyme Hall mastiffs descended from but the strain died out eventually.

The King of England, Henry VIII sent Charles V, the King of Spain around 400 mastiffs as a gift and became destined as fighting dogs. Mastiffs were also popularly used to bait a bull, lion and bear during the Elizabethan era. They were also guard dogs during the day.

Now that you know the rich history of the Mastiff breed, we will proceed on discussing the physical and behavioral aspect of the breed on the next chapter. Keep reading!

Mastiff Dogs: A Large Breed with the Heart of a Lion

Chapter One: Mastiff Physique and Temperament

English Mastiffs are fascinating – looking canines with imposing and large heads that gives the impression of having a square - ish look from every view point. These dogs have quite a grand look about them with their flat foreheads and broad heads. They sport their wrinkles whenever they are interested in something or when the dog is alert or in a defensive state. They have a well – developed cheeks and they also have large muscles on their temples. These dogs have a definite median line between their eyes that usually adds to their already imposing appearance.

Chapter One: Mastiff Physique and Temperament

In this chapter, you'll learn the physical and behavioral aspects of the English Mastiff breed including their temperament as a pet.

The English Mastiff Official Breed Standard

The muzzles of the mastiffs are short but broad under a dog's eyes. It's also blunt but with a good depth from its nose to the under – jaw. They have wide open nostrils with broad noses. Their lips are also slightly drooping but not excessively. The mastiffs also sport eyes that are moderately large and set wide apart. Their eyes are usually dark hazel in color, and they have small ears that are set wide apart on its head lying close to their cheeks when they are in a relaxed state. The Mastiff has powerful teeth and a very strong jaw.

In addition to that they also have moderately long and muscled arched necks with sloping shoulders. The front legs are strong with a good amount of bone. Their chests are wide and deep with well – rounded ribs that are also slightly arched. They also sport an extremely well – muscled loin and backs; the females have a wider area compared to the

Chapter One: Mastiff Physique and Temperament

males. Their hind legs are wide, broad and muscular with powerful back legs and developed second thighs. They have round feet with large and well – arched back nails and toes. Their tails are set high with a wider base and a tapering tip. They usually carry their tails down when relaxed but if they are excited, it usually turns into a curve with the tip pointing upwards.

When it comes to their coat, they sport a short and close – lying coat with the hair being coarser as you go over their necks and shoulders. The official breed colors of English Mastiff for the Kennel Club organization are fawn, apricot fawn and brindle.

The height of male Mastiff at the withers is 76 to 91 centimeters while their female counterparts are around 70 to 91 centimeters. The average weight of males is 68 to 113 kilogram, while females are around 54 to 82 kilogram.

When a Mastiff moves, they usually show a great amount of poise and power while walking in an easy and free gait with plenty of drive coming from their hind legs that covers a lot of ground when they move. They show total soundness as they stroll along with their keepers.

When it comes to faults, the Kennel Club don't like any form of exaggerations on the official breed standard. They will judge faults on how much it will affect a Mastiff's overall well – being and health. The main fault that comes up especially with male Mastiffs is their testicles. Both of it should fully descend on their scrotums and it's worth noting that dogs can be quite heavy or light as well as shorter or taller than what is stated in the dog's breed standard given by the Kennel Club as it is only a guideline.

Temperament

The English Mastiff breed could be quite imposing but they are gentle giants that love their owners and form strong bonds with their keeper's families. They are also fine around strangers usually to the point of being quite indifferent towards them. But expect them to quickly defend their keeper or the property they are watching if they

Chapter One: Mastiff Physique and Temperament

somehow feel that they're being threatened. This is also one of the reasons why they are quite popular guard dogs.

These dogs are best suited for people who already have some experience in handling the needs of larger dog breeds. It will be best if the household has at least one person that the Mastiff can hang around with even when everyone else is out. The reason why Mastiffs don't like being left alone especially for long periods of time is because they thrive on human connection. They must be socializing at an early age because it's much easier to train them while they're young. Part of socializing your pet includes exposing them to new people, other animals, noises, places and new situations. Once your dog has been fully vaccinated they'll surely grow up to be well – mannered, well – rounded and cool with any situation especially when they are around fellow dogs and other people.

If you will train your pet Mastiff, make sure that it's at an age where they are already manageable. As with anything else, you have to begin with the basics as soon as the pup arrives in your house. As mentioned earlier, these dogs form strong bonds with their keepers, which means

Chapter One: Mastiff Physique and Temperament

that if you left them on their own devices for too long it may result in developing separation anxiety and other behavioral issues.

Mastiffs need to be given the right amount of exercise on a daily basis but you also need to provide them with plenty of mental stimulation to keep boredom at bay otherwise this could result in them destroying your stuff at home as their way of relieving any stress that they may be feeling.

Since they are large animals, they have impressive appetites, that's given but it also means that they are quite expensive to feed. These dogs are known to slob a lot which can mean that they're not the best canine for people who want to keep everything neat. They also shed all year – round, and a Mastiff's tail that can cause a lot of damage if they wag it when they're excited. It's also worth noting that a well – bred Mastiff rarely show aggressive behavior, and is even – tempered. With this said, although imposing and big, they are also known as lazy and they can show their aloofness to strangers that they're not familiar with.

Chapter Two: Mastiff as Pets

The Mastiff breed is a smart dog and they are the kinds who like to please people. However, their training must begin as early as possible when they are still small and manageable. Their training should also be consistent and done in a fair way so that they will understand what is expected of them. Pups need to be taught the basics as soon as they arrive in your home, and once they've had all their quirks, it's also a great idea to enroll them into training classes. Enrolling them in puppy class is not only a good way to socialize your pet but also a good way to start their training in a safe and controlled area while hanging around other dog breeds and people.

Mastiff as Household Pets

Are they a good choice for first time owners?

Mastiffs may not be the best choice for first time – keepers and are better suited for keepers who already have prior experience with keeping large breeds and know their specific needs bearing in mind that they hate being left alone for long periods of time so if you and your family are always out of the house every day, then Mastiffs are not the right breed for you.

What about prey drive?

Mastiffs are very clever, and highly trainable not to chase other smaller household pets. However, they may have a high prey drive if you don't properly socialize them while they're young. An untrained Mastiff usually chase after animals that attempts to run away so make sure that

Chapter Two: Mastiff as Pets

you properly introduced them around other animals and supervise them during their interaction.

What about playfulness?

Mastiffs usually have a playful side and they love playing games with their keepers. Puppies should also be taught to place nicely so that when they grow up they will be well – mannered otherwise since they grow large and strong, they could easily knock someone if playtime becomes too rough and that's not good if you have toddlers.

What about adaptability?

Mastiffs are large dogs, which means they need to have a spacious area to express themselves. This is why they are not suitable pets for those who are living in apartments. They will be much comfy and happier if they live in large homes with gardens or backyard that they can roam around whenever they want.

What about separation anxiety?

As mentioned earlier, these dogs form strong bonds with their owners are not happy when left alone for long or even short periods of time. As such, they are better suited to keepers who can stay at home with them.

What about excessive barking?

Mastiffs are not the barker type of dog but it doesn't mean that a dog won't be quick off the mark to let their keeper know that they don't like whatever is going on around them especially if they are around strangers. But of course, if you left them alone for long periods of time, they will eventually start a barking behavior as a way of showing you that they are not happy with their situation.

Do Mastiffs like water?

Mastiff dogs know how to swim so they'll surely enjoy if you take them to nearby lakes, or beach, or if you have a swimming pool. They will love it especially if the climate is hot. However, if your pet Mastiff don't particularly like water, then don't force them to go otherwise, you'll end up scaring them. With this said, care should always be taken if you decide to walk your pet off its leash especially if it's near dangerous water courses because if your pet decides to leap in, they may not be able to get out on their own.

Are Mastiffs good watchdogs?

These dogs are natural guard dogs, thanks to their sheer size and imposing look. Those qualities alone are enough to put most burglars away especially if they are guarding a house or property. A well – bred Mastiff dog usually are protective of their homes and families but they don't show their aggressive side when they're with the people they love. Mastiffs need to be trained to be able to function as a watch dog because if not they might become dominant and show aggressive behaviors which should be avoided at all cost.

Chapter Two: Mastiff as Pets

Trainability

Training sessions are usually kept short, and this should be the same when you do it at home. It should also be interesting otherwise a pup will quickly lose their focus just like kids. If you do longer and repetitive trainings, it will be harder for your pet to keep their attention to you and what is being asked of them. Mastiffs are quite sensitive pets, and they don't respond well to any sort of harsh correction if they fail you. Positive reinforcement is best for them and giving them treats as they learn is still the best ways to make them learn.

Mastiffs need to know their place in your family's pack, and you have to show that you are the alpha dog, otherwise they will naturally take on the role of being the one who's dominant and you certainly don't want that especially since they are large dogs. All pups should also be given limitations and household rules should be set out so that your pet will know what you expect from him/ her. The most basic commands include:

- Come
- Sit
- Stay
- Quiet
- Leave it
- Down
- Bed

Reinforcement Training

When it comes to training your pup, consistency is essential. Tolerating their bad habits will only make the situation worse, and it'll be harder for you to correct them so make sure that you talk what you preach. Try seeking out a professional trainer to help you out if you have difficulties in managing your pet's behavior.

One of the first things you need to teach your pet is reward reinforcement. This method of training hinges on your dog's natural desire to please. In essence, you train your dog to repeat desired behaviors by rewarding him for doing them. For example, if you want your dog to sit, you just don't command it; you must teach him what the command means and then reward him each time he responds to the command appropriately.

Reward reinforcement training is one of the most popular and effective dog training methods. Another thing you can do is by using a clicker. This type of training is a version of reward reinforcement training and it is also highly popular. The key to success with reward reinforcement training lies in helping your dog identify the desired behavior and that is where the clicker comes in.

You go through the normal process of training, giving your dog a command and guiding him to perform the desired behavior. Then, as soon as he displays the behavior you click the clicker and immediately issue a reward; this helps your pet to learn more quickly which behavior it is that you desire. However, you should only use the clicker during the first few repetitions of a training sequence until your dog learns what the desired behavior is because you don't want him to become dependent on the clicker to perform that behavior.

Chapter Two: Mastiff as Pets

When it comes to punishment, it can also be a type of training but obviously is the opposite of reward reinforcement training. Rather than rewarding your dog for performing desired behaviors, you punish him for performing unwanted behaviors. The punishment used doesn't have to be violent or cruel. But from time to time, you can do simple punishments such as withdrawing your attention to teach your dog to stop whining. Give your dog the opposite of what he wants to curb out the negative behavior in question. This type of training is more effective as a method for curbing negative behaviors than for teaching positive behaviors.

Handling Aggression

One way of showing aggressiveness is through jumping. It is also a problem in most canine breeds especially during the adolescent stage or juvenile pups. This is a period where your pet gets so excited whenever they see people around or if other pets are nearby. They will attempt to jump on you or other animals in an effort to get your attention. Usually, jumping is a nuisance behavior and can be quite dangerous for seniors and very young kids. It can

Chapter Two: Mastiff as Pets

also be quite irritating if your Mastiff will always jumping on you or constantly knocking things off your hands.

As always, the best way is to start them while they're still young. Never reward or recognize your pup whenever they jump on you. Avoid the temptation of always trying to make them jump on you so that they will not get used to it. If you want to pet them, reach down to them or just hold them towards you, and don't do any motion or command that will provoke jumping towards you. Once your pup stops jumping, make sure to praise them or give them treats. However, if your find that jumping is part of your Mastiff's personality, what you can do is to eliminate rough plays with them such as wrestling.

You can channel your pet's playfulness towards a toy rather than you or other pets and people. Always reward your pup with a treat and a positive praise. If you have other housemates, make sure to talk to them about the behaviors that are acceptable, and those that are not so that they will not send mixed messages to your pet about the right and wrong behaviors.

Adolescent dogs are a bit harder to train than a puppy. Most of them also jump in an effort to get your attention, and if ever it wasn't corrected at a young age, jumping will become a nuisance to them. What you can do if your Mastiff is six months and older is to use a leash training method. You will need to ask another person to help you out as this requires two people.

One person must hold the dog while on a leash, and the other approaches the Mastiff. If your dog tries to jump up and greet you, what the handler should do is to tighten the leash and command the dog to sit. Do not give the dog the opportunity to jump. If your pet succeeds, both of you should praise him and give rewards. Doing this can result to a well – behaved dog and they will learn how to properly greet a person.

Children and Other Pets

Mastiff pets are laid – back by nature, and they love forming bonds with their keepers. However, because of they are generally big; they may not be the best choice if you have very young children because your pet will easily knock them out by accident especially during playtime. They tend to be great pets where the children are already older and knows how to behave around the Mastiffs. That being said, Mastiffs who grow up with kids usually form strong bonds. Supervision is needed if there are other young kids are around your own kids because they could be over – protective.

It is highly recommended that Mastiffs shouldn't be left around young kids especially babies. You have to make sure that they are never left together unattended because at the end of the day, an animal is still an animal. It's also important for parents to teach children on how to behave around large dogs as such and when to stay away especially when food is around, or when playtime gets rough.

As with other dogs, Mastiffs usually get along well with them especially if they are socialized at a young age. If a Mastiff grow up with a family cat for instance, they usually get along but supervision is still encouraged. Mastiffs may not get along with other cat breeds, and prey animals such as rabbits, hamsters and the likes so make sure to bear that in mind because your Mastiff will surely chase after them if these prey animals make a run for it.

Pros and Cons

Positives

- Mastiffs are devoted and loyal to their owners
- They are low maintenance when it comes to grooming
- They are generally good with children provided that there's supervision and proper introduction.
- They rarely show aggression but are also good guard dogs
- They are clever pets and highly trainable

Negatives

- Mastiffs are big dog breeds and can be quite expensive to feed
- They droolers and slobbers
- They tend to shed all – year round especially around spring and autumn time

Chapter Two: Mastiff as Pets

- They have a high prey drive towards other smaller prey animals
- They are family – oriented but the downside is that they can suffer from separation anxiety
- Mastiffs are not the best dog breed for first – time keepers
- They are not suitable for people living in apartments.

Chapter Three: Caring for a Mastiff

Just like any other breed, Mastiffs need to be groomed on a regular basis so that their skin and coats are kept in good condition. Keep in mind that they're prone to suffering from skin allergies, and should your pet has that make sure to treat it as soon as possible. Mastiffs also need regular exercise so that they can stay healthy and fit. On top of this, they also need to be fed with good quality food that meets all their dietary needs. In this chapter, you'll learn about how to care for them and the supplies you'll need for maintenance.

Chapter Three: Caring for a Mastiff

Caring for a Mastiff Puppy

Mastiff pups are full of life which is why you need to ensure that your homes have puppy – proof before they even arrive. If you acquire your pup from a responsible breeder, then expect that he/ she will always be confident, outgoing, curious and friendly. That being said, pups usually feel vulnerable when they leave the litter so make sure to take that into account.

It's always best to pick a pup when you or your family members are present for a week or so because the puppy will need time to settle in. Make sure that you put away any harmful tools or dangerous spots that might injure them such as cables, electric wires, toxic plants, small toys etc.

Pups need to sleep for them to properly develop and grow, so you need to set up a nice quiet area that's not too far from where you/ your family are. It's important to not disturb them while they're sleeping. It's also a good idea to keep playtime calm when they're inside the house, and give

Chapter Three: Caring for a Mastiff

them an opportunity to have an active playtime outside their gardens so that your pups will learn to behave inside.

When it comes to finding a breeder, make sure that documentation is provided for a puppy. It should include details such as worming date, information relating to their micro – chip, vaccines, food etc.

Things you'll need for your puppy

There are various items that new keepers need to prepare prior to bringing a new Mastiff pup home. It's often a good idea to also restrict the space where the pup plays in so that you can keep an eye on them. You may need to invest in puppy gates or a large enough play pen that will allow them to have some freedom while staying safe. Some puppy items include:

- Puppy gates
- Large enough playpen
- Various well – made toys that should include good quality chews that are suitable for pups to gnaw on. Keep in mind that a pup will start teething anything when they reach around 3 to 8 months old.

Chapter Three: Caring for a Mastiff

- Good quality water and feed bowls. Ideally it should be ceramic and not made out of metal or plastic
- Grooming gloves
- Soft bristle brush or slicker brush
- Dog toothbrush and toothpaste
- Scissors have rounded ends
- Nail clippers
- Puppy shampoo and conditioner
- Quality harness or dog collar
- Strong dog leads
- Quality bed that's the appropriate size
- Well – made dog crate that your pup can use at home and in the car which is also large enough for the pup to move around
- Baby blankets that you can put in your pup's crate and beds so that they'll be comfy when they take a nap or go to sleep at night

Keeping the noise down

All pups are sensitive to noise and that includes Mastiff dogs. It's essential to keep the noise levels down when a new pup arrives in their home. Music and TVs shouldn't be played too loud because it can end up stressing your pup especially if they're too young.

Chapter Three: Caring for a Mastiff

Keeping vet appointments

As mentioned earlier, Mastiff pups are usually given their first vaccinations by the breeders but they must have their follow – up shots which is now up to you to conduct. The vaccine schedule for pup is as follows (make sure to also consult your vet about this schedule if it's applicable to your pup):

- 10 to 12 weeks old. Keep in mind though that a pup wouldn't have full protection right away. It will only protect them for about 2 weeks after they've had their 2nd vaccination.

When it comes to boosters, it's also ideal to discuss it with your vet because there are lots of debates about whether a canine really needs them after a certain period of time.

What about older Mastiffs when they reach their senior years?

Adult Mastiff breeds have lots of special care as much as pups because when they reach their golden years, they are

Chapter Three: Caring for a Mastiff

also at a risk of developing certain health issues. Physically speaking, a dog's muzzle may eventually become grey but there are other noticeable changes too which could include the following:

- Coarser coats

- A loss of muscle tone

- Overweight or underweight as they age

- They have reduced stamina and strength

- Senior dogs have a hard time regulating their body temperature

- They will most likely develop arthritis

- Immune systems may not be as strong anymore as they once did making them more prone to infections and diseases.

Senior dogs also change in their mental state because it could mean that their response time tends to be slower and they may also develop the following:

Chapter Three: Caring for a Mastiff

- They may respond less to external environment due to impaired hearing and vision

- They tend to be a bit choosy in their food

- They have lower pain threshold

- They can become intolerant of any change

- They may often feel disoriented

Living with a Mastiff dog when they reach their senior years means that you will be taking a few more responsibilities but it can be easily managed. You may want to rethink their diet, the amount of exercise, their beds, and their health condition.

Older dogs should also be fed with a good quality diet that meets their nutritional needs at this stage of their lives but you have to keep a close eye on their weight. A rough feeding guide for senior Mastiffs is as follows:

- Protein content should be anything from 14 – 21%
- Fat content should be less than 10%
- Fibre content should be less than 4%

Chapter Three: Caring for a Mastiff

- Calcium content should be 0.5 – 0.8%
- Phosphorous content should be 0.4 – 0.7%
- Sodium content should be 0.2 – 0.4%

Keep in mind that they should be fed highly digestible diet that doesn't contain any additives. Senior Mastiffs shouldn't be given too much exercise but they will still need the right amount of physical activity to maintain muscle tone, and prevent them from becoming overweight. They also need to have constant access to clean water because they will also be more prone to having kidney problems.

Exercise

Mastiffs are clever dogs, and even if they are sometimes lazy or timid, you need to provide them with the right amount of exercise as well as mental stimulation so that they can be well – rounded pets. Mastiffs need a minimum of one hour exercise a day with as much off the lead as possible.

Chapter Three: Caring for a Mastiff

If you don't give them the right amount of physical and mental stimulation on a daily basis, then your pet will quickly get bored and may start showing some form of destructive behaviors around the house because this is their way of releasing their stress.

What you can do is to take them for a short stroll during the day, it's ideal to take a much longer stroll in the afternoon as well. You will often see Mastiffs just roaming around back garden or back yards because that's how they express themselves and let off steam. Just make sure to fence them in and secure it so that they won't be able to escape. These smart dogs will use their strength to find the way out so make sure to prevent that from happening.

That being said though, Mastiff pups shouldn't be over – exercised because their bones and joints are still in development stage. This also includes not letting your pet jump off high structure in the house or down the stairs. If too much pressure is placed on their spines and joints at a young age then it could result in creating serious problems later in their lives.

Average Cost to Keep and Care for a Mastiff

If you're looking to purchase a Mastiff breed, you may need to pay anything from $445 to a little over £1200 especially if you want to acquire a well – bred pedigree pup. The cost of insuring a Mastiff will vary depending on your location. Usually though, it is paid on a monthly basis. You can choose to purchase basic cover or if you want a lifetime policy which is at a premium for more pet insurance companies. These pet insurance companies factor in various things in your insurance plan, such as where you live, the age of your Mastiff, the health condition etc.

When it comes to the cost of food, you need to buy a good quality dog food (wet or dry) as long as it suits and fits the needs of your Mastiff and is appropriate for their age. This would cost you around $100 - $120 a month.

In addition to all these, you also need to think about the vet costs if you want to keep a Mastiff breed. This will also include paying for initial vaccines, annual boosters, surgical spaying or neutering, annual health checks which can cost you around $1900 a year or more.

Chapter Three: Caring for a Mastiff

As an estimate guide, the average cost to care and keep this dog would be around £150 to £210 a month depending on the supplies you'll want for your pet including emergency fund should your Mastiff needs it. However, it doesn't include the initial purchase price of a healthy and well – bred Mastiff puppy.

Knowing How a Dog was Bred

It goes without saying that sharing your life with a pet is rewarding for everyone in the family including the pet itself whether it's a dog, cat or other household animals. For kids, it is a great way to learn about the value of responsibility when they need to care for another pup. Keep in mind though that children should also have a positive experience when it comes to household pets, make sure that you supervise them at all times to avoid any mishaps.

It is pretty rare for dogs especially Mastiffs to attack children but it still happens so make sure as a parent and as a responsible dog keeper that you understand the reasons why sometimes aggression happens so that you'll know how to prevent such circumstance.

Chapter Three: Caring for a Mastiff

There are times when dogs are misunderstood by their keepers which results to having a companion that don't get enough physical and mental stimulation. In other type of breeds it can be quite dangerous due to their high prey drive.

Another issue is that many breeds are not properly trained and some of them are even encouraged by their owners to show their aggressive nature. If there's too much interaction between the owner and the dog that involves raising voices or shouting, it will eventually affect a dog's behavior and make them an aggressive pet.

Young children usually have no fear whenever they see a dog around even if the dog is showing aggression. This will make them more at risk of being bitten or have a traumatic experience which involves a dog growling at them. If an adult is not around, this can be very dangerous to the child.

It's essential to know where and how a canine was bred even if knowing their parentage can be quite difficult especially if you just adopted them from a rescue centre.

Chapter Three: Caring for a Mastiff

Pups that were not trained or socialized can develop more behavioral issues as they grow into adulthood. This may include aggressiveness towards other kids because they find themselves in an unfamiliar situation. Aggression is usually caused by the dog's insecurity.

Dogs and Children

When dogs and kids are together, there are times when their behaviors tend to clash. This is especially true of toddlers and very young children. Kids who have grown up around household pets eventually learn how to behave around them but it's very important to still supervise them when they are interacting with dogs.

It would be fair to say that a lot of canines find it hard to be around very small children and even the gentlest giants like the Mastiff breed can get stressed out. Also, large dogs like the Mastiff are also prone to knocking small kids especially during playtime when it gets rough. This kind of situation could negatively impact a kid so make sure to not leave them alone together.

Chapter Three: Caring for a Mastiff

There are cases when kids have facial injuries and many people think that it happened because of the kid's height or because they made direct eye contact with the dog causing them to get bitten. This can be seen as a threatening behavior and usually the dog's natural reaction is to retaliate. That being said, your kids may be at risk of being bitten if you allow them to play on the floor with your pet which can turn an innocent game into an unfortunate incident.

Children move too fast

Sometimes dogs find it hard to cope with young kids that move too fast, your pup may find it unsettling especially if it's coupled with high pitch scream. It can sometimes stress dogs, and may snap or nip at the child. However, most dogs usually give some kind of warning before they attempt to snap, it's usually a growl or they may even be the one to distance themselves from the child.

Children tease dogs

If children are left on their own, they may innocently tease your Mastiff, and this could result the dog being frustrated. The unfortunate thing is that the child may be too

Chapter Three: Caring for a Mastiff

young to recognize the warning signs that the dog is already exhibiting making them more at risk of being bitten or snap at. This is usually the dog's way of trying to stop people or other animals from teasing them.

Children hurt dogs without knowing it

Young kids are still learning the ropes when it comes to interacting with pets, and they can hurt a dog accidentally by maybe hugging them too tight or maybe getting right in front of their face. If ever the child gets bitten by dogs, this can be a traumatic experience and the child may remain scared of the dogs for the rest of their lives.

Feeding

If you acquired your Mastiff pup from a breeder, they usually give you the pup's feeding schedule. It's very important to stick to this feeding schedule so as not to cause any stomach upset on your puppy. You may change your dog's diet but it should be done in a very gradual way and make sure that they don't develop any type of digestive problems once they eat a different diet. If problems arise, it's

Chapter Three: Caring for a Mastiff

always best to put them back on their original diet and consult your vet before changing their meals again.

Adult dogs are quite fussy eaters especially as they reach their senior years but it doesn't mean that you should feed them a low – quality meal. It is better to feed your adult Mastiff twice a day, one in the morning and in the evening. Make sure that what you offer them meets all their nutritional needs. It's also best to give them the right amount of exercise so that they can burn off any excess calories and prevent them from gaining too much weight as this can lead to health issues. Obesity is a silent killer for most dogs so make sure to pay attention to what they consume from the get – go.

Mastiff dogs are known to suffer from bloat so make sure to just feed them twice a day and don't give it just one large meal for a day. It's also best to invest in a stand wherein you can put their feed bowls making it easier for your large Mastiff to eat - this way your pet will be comfortable during eating time and not need to stretch their necks out just to reach their food. You should also not exercise your dog before or just after they have eaten their

Chapter Three: Caring for a Mastiff

meals otherwise it can cause them to suffer from gastric torsion. Bloat is a serious condition that can also be fatal for dogs. If your pet suffer from this and show signs of gastric torsion, make sure to bring him/her to the vet ASAP.

Feeding Guide for a Mastiff Puppy

Pups need to be fed with good quality dog food that's also highly nutritious because this is the stage where they need to develop. Your Mastiff pup can be fed the following amounts on a daily basis, making sure that their meals are spread out throughout the day. It's also ideal to feed them thrice or four times a day:

- 2 months old: 319g to 547g depending on build of the puppy
- 3 months old: 416g to 730g depending on build of the puppy
- 4 months old: 459g to 809g depending on build of the puppy
- 5 months old: 544g to 972g depending on build of the puppy

Chapter Three: Caring for a Mastiff

- 6 months old: 617g to 1104g depending on build of the puppy
- 7 months old: 619g to 1124g depending on build of the puppy
- 8 months old: 615g to 1129g depending on build of the puppy
- 9 months old: 567g to 1293g depending on build of the puppy
- 10 months old: 531g to 1248g depending on build of the puppy
- 11 months old: 486g to 1011g depending on build of the puppy
- 12 months old: 444g to 961g depending on build of the puppy
- 13 months old: 441g to 904g depending on build of the puppy
- 14 months old: 436g to 851g depending on build of the puppy
- Once your pup reaches 18 months, you can start feeding them adult dog food.

Chapter Three: Caring for a Mastiff

Feeding guide for an adult Mastiff

When your Mastiff reaches its full maturity, make sure to feed him/her a good quality diet so that they will continue to be healthy. Here's a rough guide of how much you can feed your pet but it's also ideal to consult the vet as this could vary depending on the dog's needs:

- Dogs weighing 54 kg can be fed 458g to 519g depending on activity
- Dogs weighing 68 kg can be fed 519g to 683g depending on activity
- Dogs weighing 82 kg can be fed 635g to 836g depending on activity
- Dogs weighing 113 kg can be fed 739g to 984g depending on activity

Grooming

Mastiffs have short and close coats that are low – maintenance grooming wise. You can just brush your pet at least once a week and wipe it with a chamois leather to ensure that their coats will be kept in good condition. Keep in mind though that Mastiffs shed on a steady basis year –

round particularly during spring and autumn so you need to do more frequent brushing during these periods to remove any loose hair from your pet's coat.

It's also best to always check your dog's ears and clean them when necessary, this is because if too much wax builds up on your pet's ears it may lead to infection and can be more difficult to clean. When it comes to your Mastiff's hygiene, prevention is also better than cure.

Chapter Four: Mastiff Buying Advice

As a potential owner, it is up to you to ensure that the pup you acquire is healthy and is responsibly bred. This is why it's important that you have some kind of checklist when making a decision to buy especially when deciding from whom to buy. When purchasing a Mastiff puppy or dog, there are various things to consider and questions that you need to ask to your prospective breeder. Mastiffs are quite popular breeds which means that well – bred pups could be expensive. There are protocols, advice and questions to follow if you want to acquire a purebred

Chapter Four: Mastiff Buying Advice

Mastiff. Read on to know how to find a reputable breeder and a healthy Mastiff puppy.

Before You Buy

Beware of scammers.

There are lots of ads online but usually they are scammers so you have to be very careful. Scammers often show images of cute Mastiff litters for sale at very cheap prices. One way of knowing that they are a scammer is when they ask you to give them money up front before agreeing to deliver a pup to your house. Buyers should never purchase a pup or any other animal without first seeing it and the environment it grew up in. You should also not pay an initial deposit without getting the pup first. Make sure to visit the pet first to confirm if the litter is a Mastiff breed and ask them the necessary questions.

Check if the breeder is reputable

Mastiff are among the most popular breeds in the world which is why you may find lots of backyard breeders or hobbyists who breed their pets far too often just so they

Chapter Four: Mastiff Buying Advice

can make a quick buck without caring for the puppies and the dam's welfare. There are rules when it comes to breeding, one of which is that dams should ideally produce only four litters and she must be at the right age. Anyone that's wishing to buy a pup should consider if the breeder is reputable and you should always ask for the necessary paperwork pertaining to the lineage of the puppy, micro – chipping and records of vaccinations.

Other Factors to Consider

Do your research first

Before you inquire to a seller or visit a breeder, make sure that you know what you're getting into. You have to do your research first, and learn all about the Mastiff breed, or any other breed you're considering before you make a final decision. It's important to read the profile of the breed and all the details you need to know relevant to keeping that particular breed, in this case the Mastiff, before you proceed.

Chapter Four: Mastiff Buying Advice

Confirm that the advertiser is genuine

When it comes to arranging to visit a puppy or a dog, what you need to check out is the kind of environment where the breed is raised. There might be breeders that will let you check out the dog at another address where both of you can meet halfway or something, and he/she will just bring the pet along; the downside to this is that you never know how the puppy is raised even if you see the breed in person. Never accept an offer to have the puppy just delivered to your home, and you shouldn't also pay upfront nor do an online payment because if you happen to interact with a scammer and you pay online, they could steal your credit card information.

Is the puppy over 8 weeks of age?

Puppies should be at least around eight weeks old and fully weaned before they can be purchased. Some breeders especially those who are registered under certain kennel club associations, don't let their pups go to new homes until they reach twelve weeks old so that's also ideal. We highly encourage you to find a breeder that insists on

Chapter Four: Mastiff Buying Advice

this because that's usually a good sign that he/ she is a reputable breeder.

Check the health of the puppy or dog

While it can be a bit difficult for non – breeders to spot a potential illness in the puppy or dog especially during the first interaction, you should have an agreement with the seller that after you make a purchase, you can still return the breed within 48 hours if a vet found out that the breed have hereditary health problems or is not in good condition. Getting your Mastiff dog checked out by the vet after having them will ensure that everything will go smooth moving forward.

Can the puppies be viewed with their mother?

Make sure that if you view the litter, you also visit the mother and father of the breed, or at least one of the parents. Seeing the parent breed/s will give you an insight into the kind of traits and temperament the puppy could have as they grow older. If the mother dog is not available to be seen, then the breeder may not be reputable. Consider this a warning sign.

Chapter Four: Mastiff Buying Advice

Is the puppy or dog up to date with their vaccinations?

Puppies need to have two – stage vaccine shots before they'd be allowed to go outside. The first vaccine shot should be around eight to ten weeks old, and the second shot should be two weeks later. These vaccine shots are often done by the breeder due to the puppies' weaning age. As a potential owner, you will be responsible for the succeeding vaccines that your pet will need after the first two. The vaccines should also be up to date. Make sure to ask the vaccination card of the puppy or have a record of your pet's vaccination status; the breeder where you acquire it should have the proof of the first one or two vaccine shots.

Have the puppies been treated for worms and fleas?

Puppies can already be treated for worms and fleas when they already reached two weeks old. Reputable breeders use the right product from a young age. If the puppy is properly cared for then there's no reason why he/she should have worms or fleas so make sure to check this and take it as a warning sign if the puppy hasn't been treated for worms or fleas.

Chapter Four: Mastiff Buying Advice

Is the puppy/dog micro - chipped?

Since April 2016, pups that are over eight weeks old are required by law to be micro – chipped and it's also mandatory for the breeder or keeper to keep the details up to date. This only means that if you purchase a pup, they already need to have a micro – chip implanted in accordance with the law. Make sure to verify it, check the paperwork and get a copy of the necessary documents from the breeder before buying the pup. If the puppy is not yet micro – chipped then consider it as a warning sign that the breeder you're dealing with is not reputable.

Ask questions about the puppies' mother

Find out the dam's temperament, her age, the litters she had and why she's chosen for breeding (health – wise). These things will help tell you about the mother of the pups and how the breeder raised her as well.

Chapter Four: Mastiff Buying Advice

Is the dog/puppy registered with The Kennel Club?

If the puppy is registered with a certain kennel organization whether it is AKC in the U.S., or The Kennel Club in the U.K., make sure that the documents for the dog is in order and prepared. Never accept an explanation that the papers will be sent at a later time.

Have the puppies been socialized?

Puppies should already have an initial interaction with the world around them especially to other people and pets. This will naturally happen if the puppies are raised in a suitable home environment. If they are not raise in a good environment they will likely have behavioral problems or have trouble adjusting to a new home. It will make them harder to train and manage.

Chapter Five: Mastiff Health and Caring Tips

The average life span of a Mastiff is around 10 to 12 years old. If you properly care for your pet and feed him/her the right nutrition and quality diet that's appropriate for their age then you can be almost certain that they'll live a happy and long life. However, just like any other breeds, these dogs are also susceptible to some health issues. Mastiffs suffer from a few hereditary issues which are worth knowing for you as the keeper. If you're planning to share a home with these large and imposing dogs, then taking care of their health is part of the package.

Chapter Five: Mastiff Health and Caring Tips

Common Health Issues of Mastiffs

The most common health issues that affect the Mastiff breed include the following:

- Hip Dysplasia: breeders should have their stud dogs tested for hip score

- Elbow Dysplasia: breeders should have their stud dogs tested for hip score

- Progressive Retinal Atrophy: breeders should have their stud dogs eye tested through an Animal Health Trust

- Pyometra

- Wobbler syndrome

- Bone cancer

- Kidney stones

- Allergies

- Canine acne

- Cranial cruciate ligament injury

- Canine cystinuria

- Obesity

- Bloat - gastric torsion

What about vaccinations?

Mastiff pups should have already been given an initial vaccine before a breeder sells it out. As a keeper, it is up to you to ensure that your dog take their follow – up shots and follow the schedule that was recommended by your dog's vet. In general the vaccination schedule for pups should be when they are 10 to 12 weeks old. This way the puppy will be fully – protected for two weeks after they've had their second vaccine.

When it comes to boosters, there's been quite a lot of debate whether or not dogs need it. As such, we highly recommend that you consult your vet before you make a decision on whether you want your Mastiff pup to continue with boosters (annual vaccinations).

What about spaying and neutering?

There are lots of vets today that recommend waiting until the breed are slightly older before neutering or spaying them. You may need to wait until your Mastiff pup reach a certain point of physical maturity before you let him/ her go through surgical procedures. As such, many vets advise spaying females and neutering males when they're around 6 to 9 months old, or once they reach one year old.

There are also vets that recommend spaying and neutering canines when they're just six months old, but it shouldn't be any earlier unless there's a medical reason. That being said, individual dog breeds are different, and it's always best to discuss these with your vet and follow their advice.

What about obesity problems?

There are Mastiffs that gain weight after they've been neutered or spayed and it's essential to keep an eye on your pet's waistline just in case they do. If your pet starts to put on some weight, then you have to do your part and adjust

Chapter Five: Mastiff Health and Caring Tips

their daily caloric intake, and perhaps increase the amount of physical activity that your dog is currently engaged in. Older Mastiffs usually are susceptible to becoming overweight which is why it's very important that they get fed accordingly and get the right amount of exercise because obesity can definitely shorten your pet's life by many years. The reason for this is because it puts on a lot of extra strain on the dog's internal organs particularly their heart and kidneys.

What about allergies?

Mastiffs are also prone to allergies, which is why it's best for your pet to see a vet sooner rather than later so that it can be prevented or treated right away before it gets worse. Allergies can be very difficult to clear up and finding its triggers can also be challenging. Your vet will be able to make a dog with an allergy more comfortable while they try to find out the triggers such as airborne pollens, flea and tick bites, chemicals in household cleaning products, dust mites, and overall environment.

Participating in health schemes

If you acquire your pet from a responsible breeder, then there's some form of assurance that their stud dogs are tested as there could be hereditary or congenital health issues that have been known to affect the Mastiffs. The test includes hip scoring for hip dysplasia and elbow dysplasia as well as eye tests for possible progressive retinal atrophy condition.

What about breed specific breeding restrictions?

In addition from the standard breeding restrictions that were set out for all Kennel Club registered breeds, there are no further specific breeding restrictions that are set out for the Mastiff.

What about Assured Breeder Requirements?

It's mandatory for some kennel organizations to have their stud dogs tested for the hip dysplasia scheme. We highly recommend that all Mastiff breeders use the following schemes on all dogs destined to be used for breeding purposes; this includes the elbow dysplasia scheme, bitches that are under 20 months old should not be bred yet, and bitches over six years shouldn't produce a litter.

Testing For Hip Dysplasia in Dogs

Hip dysplasia is a condition that leads to abnormal hip development. It is a hereditary issue that affected many dog breeds including Mastiffs. Hip dysplasia can be very painful for your pet and can certainly affect their mobility. And because this condition is passed on from one generation to another, preventing dogs with this condition from breeding is very important. For instance, the Kennel Club organization requires breeder from not breeding pedigree of dogs with bad hips.

Affected dogs may need quite a complicated surgery to correct this kind of condition, but it's not possible in all cases. The best way to manage this hip dysplasia condition in your Mastiff is through testing him/ her for this condition especially if you plan on breeding your pet as this will ensure that other dogs will not become carriers and will not be used for breeding.

What is hip dysplasia?

Hip dysplasia can affect one or both hips of your pet and it usually occurs when their hips don't develop properly as they go through the transition from being a pup to an adult which means that there are cases wherein the condition doesn't become apparent or seen until your pet reaches around two years old.

In healthy hips, the ball and socket joints fit together and are well – match as this will allow the dog to have a proper range of movement without experiencing pain or mobility problems. If a dog has hip dysplasia, their joints develop abnormally which means that the socket and ball joints don't perfectly fit together. This is often exacerbated by poor muscle tone around the dog's hip joint which also helps keeping it in place for healthy dog breeds.

Affected dogs are usually born with normal hips and it doesn't cause them any problems until when they get a bit older. Over time, the socket and ball joint of affected dogs

Chapter Five: Mastiff Health and Caring Tips

will begin to separate and this separation will cause the hips to become malformed and painful for your Mastiff making them unable to move properly. Vets also refer to this as subluxation.

Testing for Hip Dysplasia

A hip dysplasia test will help keepers and vets identify a pre – disposition. This test is called hip scoring and it results in the person assessing the state of the dog's hips. There will be some scoring metric which will indicate how healthy or not they are relative to the disease.

The scoring system of hip dysplasia runs from 0 to 106. The lower the score, the better the hip health of your dog. Each breed of dog has a hip score average so that means that it can vary between canines. The umbrella guidance for breeding is to only breed from canines whose hip score is below the average for that particular breed.

Scoring is usually carried out by a professional. It involves an X – ray of the dog's hips which will then be taken to your local vet clinic and make send it off for assessment.

What types of dogs are prone to hip dysplasia?

Hip dysplasia is one of the most common genetic skeletal condition that affect dog breeds. Lots of dog breeds are at risk of this health condition. Make sure to be informed about the recommended health test for the Mastiff breed from your respective dog register. Large dog breeds like St. Bernard and German Shepherd are usually at greater risk compared to smaller dog breeds but then again, it can be present in most canines including cross breeds.

What sort of dogs should be tested for the condition?

The sort of pedigree dogs that are listed by kennel organizations usually include those who are at more risk, they advise that these dog breeds be tested under the KC/BVA scheme prior to breeding them. There are dog breeds that are at particular high risk of the hip dysplasia, it's actually needed if you want to register your pet officially to kennel organizations.

Dogs that have a known history of this health issue in their breed line whether or not the dog appears healthy

Chapter Five: Mastiff Health and Caring Tips

should still be tested especially if you are planning to breed them, regardless if the condition is prevalent within the Mastiff breed.

And because scoring for the hip dysplasia condition is based on X – ray exams and it doesn't become noticeable until the canine is fully grown, hip scoring can only be applied to breeds that are above two years of age so that the test results will be definitive.

What this means is that the potential parent dogs should already be tested rather than their future litter. Both the sire and dam should be tested. The hip score results are already the score in the dog's life time, so testing and assessment will only be performed once regardless of the number of litters they will produce.

Mastiff Dog Hereditary Health and Health Testing

The Mastiffs are large dogs that are both tall and heavy. They naturally need a garden and large backyard in order to express themselves. The word Mastiff is actually quite confusing for some because this term is also widely

Chapter Five: Mastiff Health and Caring Tips

used to refer to a range of other mastiff dog breeds as well as referring to the generic Mastiff canine itself.

The term is also used interchangeably with the word molosser which is why any dog breed that falls under this dog category may be considered to be a Mastiff breed as well.

The combined height, weight and power of Mastiff dogs make them one of the largest of all dog breed. They can stand up to around 30 inches tall at the withers and can have a weight of up to 110 kilograms. Male Mastiffs are larger than females but don't be fooled because females are also large in their own right.

This canine has heavy body, huge head, deep and wide chest, and also has a square build. Mastiffs have close – lying and short coats, and they also sport a fawn or brindle marking on their faces. They are quiet and slow – moving dogs that form strong bonds with their owners. But because of their size and power, they require a keeper that's confident to manage them. As mentioned in previous chapters, they are not ideal for first – time dog keepers. In

Chapter Five: Mastiff Health and Caring Tips

this section, we will delve more about their health background and issues.

Genetic diversity within the breed

The co – efficient of inbreeding statistic for the Mastiff canine is 13.3%. This is high and it also indicates that the breed is subjected to a high degree of inbreeding. 6.25% is the ideal rate for pedigree dog breeds, and the job of breeders is to reduce the percentage within their own breed lines.

Conformation

The weight and overall size of the Mastiff breed means that their joints and legs are under a reasonable amount of pressure which is why care should be taken particularly with young pups to ensure that they don't overexert because at this stage their joints and bones are still in the process of developing.

The skin folds of the face needs drying and regular cleaning so that there wouldn't be a build – up of dirt and debris as this could lead to infections. The deep chest of the breed also places them at risk of gastric torsion or commonly known as bloat which is a digestive condition that fills their stomach with gas and can potentially flip over on itself.

Health testing

In order to ensure that the risk of hereditary health problems are kept at a minimum, there are some organizations or dog registers that recommends a wide – range of pre – breeding health tests to ensure that the next generation of puppies are healthier than their parent breeds. Here are some of the general health schemes that most registers recommend for Mastiff breed. This is also applicable to other dog breeds:

- Hip score tests. Potential breeding stock should have a hip score that's below a certain figure depending on the breed of dog you have.
- Elbow dysplasia (the ideal score is zero)
- DNA testing for progressive retinal atrophy of the eyes
- DNA testing for multi -focal retinopathy
- Bitches that are under 20 months old should not be used for breeding.

Chapter Five: Mastiff Health and Caring Tips

The Mastiff breed is classified as a high – profile by most dog registers but this also means that they are monitored due to the various hereditary health issues that can affect the breed.

Other Health Issues

The Mastiff breed as a whole also suffers from other health issues that currently don't have testing schemes in place. The health issues include:

- Osteosarcoma
- Lymphoma
- Ectropion or entropion of the eyelids – this causes the eyelids to turn outwards and inwards.
- Cystinuria – this issue may lead to bladder stones and kidney stones
- Vaginal prolapse – this usually occurs in young bitches of the breed
- Atopy – this is a type of skin allergy to certain protein particles such as pollens
- pulmonic stenosis and mitral dysplasia which are types of heart disease

Chapter Five: Mastiff Health and Caring Tips

- Canine acne – this usually affects the muzzle area of dogs.
- Cruciate ligament rupture – this condition affects the hind quarters.
- Panosteitis – this is an inflammatory condition on the bones of the dog
- Osteochondrosis – affects the shoulder and knee area.
- Cherry eye and cataracts

Chapter Six: Breeding Mastiff

When it comes to breeding, it's best to find a suitable sire that can help your bitch to conceive. The duration of pregnancy in dogs is nine weeks or sixty days. This is the period where a future litter will develop from just a few cells to cute little Mastiff puppies that are ready to play with you. Breeding is not an easy job but if you would one day go down this road, we'll cover that for you and give you some guidelines to follow in this chapter so that you will know what to expect starting from courting, mating, gestation period, labor process and so forth. We'll also give you a week by week pregnancy guide that can help you understand what happens during the gestation period.

Chapter Six: Breeding Mastiff

Gestation Period Calendar

First Week: Days 0 to 7

This is where mating, ovulation and fertilization happen. This is the time where your bitch needs to mate with the sire but keep in mind that you may need to mate the parent breeds more than once to ensure that fertilization will occur. The countdown to birth starts when the ovulation process occurs but it can be hard to monitor ovulation independently, you will need to test the body temperature of the bitch on a daily basis. One way of knowing if there's a successful mating is when the bitch starts to show some signs of morning sickness just like how it is with women. Make sure to watch out for any potential signs of infection too as she could have gotten this during mating. You may see a pink discharge from your bitch's vagina but it may not be present as well. If you do see it, be informed that this is normal.

Make sure to keep the feeding and exercise routine but you should also consider adding a nutritional supplement. You need to consult with your vet so that you can know what your bitch needs. Keep in mind to not use any worm or flea treatments during this period without first asking your vet about it.

Second Week: Days 7 to 14

This is now the second week which means that cells have already develops into the future litter. They will now become separate and tiny embryos will descend into the uterus where it will begin to grow for the whole duration of the gestation period. By this time, your bitch should still be fed and exercised following her needed routine.

Third Week: Days 14 to 21

The third week of gestation is when the embryos will start to be implanted into the uterus. This is where the future litter will receive the life support and essential nutrients which the mother will provide during the entire time that they will be on the womb. The fetus pups are under a centimeter long during this stage.

Chapter Six: Breeding Mastiff

When it comes to feeding and exercise, just follow their normal routine but you can now start monitoring your bitch if she has an increased appetite. You can provide for her growing needs accordingly, just keep in mind to not make any unnecessary or sudden diet changes. Consult the vet and do it gradually if needed.

Fourth Week: Days 21 to 28

Towards the end of the fourth week, experience breeders or the vet can already detect the developing puppies through palpating the mother's abdomen in a gentle way. This is the period where the spine and eyes of the fetuses starts to develop and their faces also begin to form. The litter grows to around 1 ½ centimeters individually during the fourth week. The breasts of the mother may also start to swell at this stage and she might also have a thin and clear discharge from her vagina.

The fourth week of fetal development is considered as the first formative stage of your bitch's pregnancy. This is the time when the pups are at most vulnerable to damage and developing defects. During this stage, make sure to not have any rough play or strenuous exercises. You need to also consult your vet about the changing nutritional needs of your pet and ask the vet if you need to provide any supplements.

Fifth Week: Days 28 to 35

This is where amniotic fluid in the mother's uterus starts to increase; its main function is to protect the litter when it reaches around the 32nd day of gestation which means you or your vet won't be able to detect the pups through the abdominal palpation. The fifth week is where pups are less prone to defects and developmental issues. This is when their toes will start to form; whisker and claws will start to grow as well. This is also when fetuses develop their sex.

Your bitch's weight will begin to noticeably increase at this stage, and you should increase her food rations now if you have not done so already. Feed little and often, and start to introduce your chosen puppy food into the mix.

Chapter Six: Breeding Mastiff

If you have decided to have an ultrasound scan done on your bitch during pregnancy to try and ascertain the number of puppies and identify any problems, this is usually performed during the fifth week.

Sixth Week: Days 35 to 42

You will now notice that your bitch will have a larger tummy and the pregnancy will also be obvious to most people. You can expect that they will now have a puppy bump and this will continue to grow on a daily basis. The nipples will also become darker as days pass by. This is the time when puppies starts to have skin pigmentation, markings, and eventually their coat color and looks.

You will need to increase the food of your bitch and provide her with as much as she wants. You need to also increase the ratio of puppy food in her diet and include multi – vitamin supplements.

This is the time to start preparing the nesting bed which the mother will use for whelping. You need to make it comfy and inviting for her; make sure it is well – padded as

Chapter Six: Breeding Mastiff

well. You also need to decide where you want to place the box for the birth and first few days of the litter while encouraging your dog to start sleeping there.

Seven Weeks: Days 42 to 49

Your bitch will start shedding the hair on her tummy at this stage as part of the birth preparation. You don't need to be alarmed because this is perfectly normal. The pups will continue developing and growing, and by this time they will almost completely become fully – formed.

At the end of the 7th week, you need to stop feeding puppy food and go back to feeding the regular nutritious diet – again, as much as she wants to. This will trigger the mother's body to start storing calcium acquired from the puppy food that's been fed to her up to this point – this is an important mineral during the later stages of your pet's pregnancy.

Eight Weeks: Days 49 to 57

Chapter Six: Breeding Mastiff

You can expect the bitch to give birth at any time from this week onwards. Make sure to avoid any rough play or stimulation that might lead to the onset of early labor since ideally the litter still needs another week inside the womb. Your dog will now begin nesting at the eight week, and you may also see or feel the litter moving inside her tummy when she's lying down.

The mother will also start producing colostrums at this point; the forerunner to her nutrient – rich milk before the milk itself. Continue to feed as much as your bitch wants to eat and you should also start preparing for her birth.

Ninth Week: Days 57 to 65

This is the last week of pregnancy which means that you should be ready because your dog will certainly give birth within the ninth week. She will also become more introverted as she prepares for the birth of her litter. You need to feed as much as your bitch wants but also be ready for her appetite may drop when whelping gets closer and closer.

You should start taking your bitch's temperature more than twice a day. If the pregnancy progresses past the 60th day, you should check it every few hours every day and night so that you can identify the impending onset of labor.

Getting Ready For Birth

Deciding to breed your Mastiff entails that there are lots of things to think about and this includes preparing for whelping. As whelping draws near with each passing day, it's essential that you fully – prepare since that's what responsible keepers do. You need to have everything you need that can help your dog during the birthing process.

Whether this is your first – time breeding a dog or you already have some experience, you're going to have a lot in your mind as your pet undergo the labor process. You need to have a handy list of the kit that your dog will need and some guidelines to follow as these can be invaluable in making sure that everything will go well for your dog, and that you will keep stress at a minimum for you.

Chapter Six: Breeding Mastiff

Have a Plan B

As whelping gets nearer and nearer, you need to have an emergency plan in place. In other words, you need to have a Plan B. Here are some tips:

- You need to have your vet's phone number including a number for out – of – hours – cover and he/ she should be aware of your pet's impending birth. If ever your vet won't be available at the time when your dog gives birth or is about to give birth, then make sure to have the veterinary records with you so that you can have some guide.
- You need to also prepare your car or any transportation at hand just in case you would need to take your dog to a surgeon if ever she runs into labor problems.
- If you don't own a car or transportation won't be available, then you may need to find a way on how to get to a nearby clinic. You can also try to ask help from another dog breeder who already have an experienced and have him/ her on call should you need it.

- If you have other household pets or kids that you need to care for, then make sure to assign someone who can look after them, may it be a sitter, friend, or a relative, so that you can have the time and attention to accompany your dog during the labor process.

Prepare the Whelping Box

Your whelping box is the place where the mother will give birth. This will also be the temporary home of the litter for the first three weeks of their lives. The whelping box should be large enough for the litter and also for the mother.

She should be able to sit comfortably, stretch her legs out and turn around if she wants to. It should also have walls around the sides that are high enough to keep the pups from crawling off but it should also have easy access for the mother to get in and out. You will also need to provide pads both on the sides and floor of the box so that it will be comfortable for the bitch and her litter. Make sure to have a spare bedding because you may need to change their bedding on a regular basis or as needed. Keep some old cloth and newspaper to use for whelping because it will surely get messy once your dog gets into labor. You should also keep hot water bottles that are securely wrapped to prevent the bitch and her pups from getting burned. You can also use heat pads for the litter to keep them warm.

Whelping Materials

Keep in mind that dogs and animals in general are unaided when they give birth in the wild, which is why the role you will play as your pet gives birth will be minimal unless of course an issue arise. Dogs of some breeds are more likely to need help when it comes to giving birth particularly breeds with large heads. Your Mastiff may need some type of assistance or she may undergo through a caesarean section for her to deliver the pups.

Some dogs need to have a caesarean section or surgery and this include breeds like boxer dogs or those with squashed – up faces. A good example is the bull dog breed because 80% of the litters are usually delivered through caesarean section. If this is what your pet's needs, then you'll have to plan for this and consult with your dog's

Chapter Six: Breeding Mastiff

vet well in advance so that your dog will have a smooth delivery.

If you have decided during the consultation with the vet that your dog will give birth at home, then you should some equipment on hand, and have it prepared before the labor starts. You need to rely on your own when it comes to deciding when and how you will use it to aid during the birthing process. If this is your first – time and you're not yet confident with your abilities, it's best that you have an experienced breeder with you that can help and guide you, or do it with your vet around. Here are some of the things your dog might need:

- Haemostatic clamps: this can be used to crimp the umbilical cord
- Clean scissors: this cutting the umbilical cord
- Surgical gloves
- Warm towels: this can be use to rub and wrap the new puppies
- Lubricant that's approved by your vet (ex: KY jelly)
- Thermometer: this will be needed to monitor your dog's temperature before she gives birth. Make sure

to take down notes so that you can properly monitor it.

- Paper collars: this will allow you to easily identify each pup after birth
- A weighing scale: you will need to accurately record the birth weight of each of the pup. You can use a digital kitchen scale which can cover a suitable range of weights.
- Milk Substitute: Your puppies will need this and you can actually order it from your vet. You will also need a bottle and teat with the right dimensions so that it could properly be administered to this to the puppies.
- Calcium supplement: this is for the bitch during her birth as this will support the parathyroid gland in releasing the necessary hormones that will enable them to push easier.
- Water and food: this is for the mother especially after the labor process. You can also include a high energy supplemental drink or a nutritious broth because it will aid in your bitch's needs before and after giving birth. Make sure to consult with your vet so that you will know the best choice for your pet.

Chapter Six: Breeding Mastiff

Take care of yourself

As the birth of the litter draws nearer, you will do lots of things like monitoring your bitch regularly on a daily basis such as taking her body temperature and also checking if there are any signs of distress. You may want to be comfortable yourself during this time. We suggest that you use some pillows, bean bag or sleeping bags at ground level that you can stay in so that you will be close at hand to attend to your pet's needs. Take care yourself and make sure that you eat regularly and keep yourself hydrated especially if your dog's labor lasts for quite a long period of time. Keep in mind that you won't be able to help your dog be at her best during this time if you yourself are not at your best.

The First Stages of Labor

Are you and your bitch read for this? Your bitch is now comfortable, your whelping box is there and all the materials are ready; you already learned some protocols just in case your dog encounter some problems, now what?

Chapter Six: Breeding Mastiff

Identifying the impending onset of labour

As labor day for your dog gets closer, you need to be monitoring her temperature several times in a day. If the body temperature of the bitch drops around 38 to 37 degrees Celsius up to 36.5 degrees, then that means that she can give birth within the next 24 hours. Another sign to look out for is the change of behavior. If you see your bitch getting more and more uncomfortable then that means that she's very near to giving birth. Here are some behavioral changes prior to labor:

- Your dog will start losing her appetite
- She may become too clingy and doesn't like to be left alone
- You may notice a light discharge from her vagina. The outward appearance of your dog's back end may also become more prominent.
- Your bitch's pupils may become dilated and bigger and she may appear to be staring
- Your dog may become restless; if you notice that your pet get up and down a lot or she's very uncomfortable then that means she's close.

Chapter Six: Breeding Mastiff

- You may see her constantly seeking out her whelping box or going to a quiet spot where she can be comfortable.

Some dogs will display all of these signs while some may not, just be alert when her behavior suddenly changes so that you can prepare for it and care for her.

What happens next?

As the early stages of labor starts, your dog will eventually decide as to where she would want to give birth. Some dogs choose the whelping box but some don't. You have to prepare if she would pick a spot where she would be comfortable but not inside the whelping box. Some dogs start digging around the box or within their chosen area, while some will start re – arranging the bedding or do something else. Just let her does what she wants and don't intervene. You need to let the bitch be comfortable in her own way.

You may see her pay a lot of attention at her vulva, and may start to lick it; this usually indicates that something

Chapter Six: Breeding Mastiff

is happening. You may also see her shivering or catching her breath but this is totally normal and not a cause for concern. This may mean that your pet is experiencing the first stages of mild contractions and you may not notice it until it becomes more frequent and also stronger. There's also a possibility that she'll start vomiting, urinating or defecating.

You may also see a mucous discharge coming out of her vulva and it's almost certainly present by this point as her body prepares for birth. This mucous discharge usually looks like a clear fluid or a milky one. If you see that the discharge is color yellow or green, you may need to contact your vet. This is because a green discharge is not normal before birth; it only becomes normal after giving birth to the first pup.

When you finally notice the first contractions, it's time to offer your dog a calcium rich food/ drink or supplement that your vet recommended because this will help support her during the labor process and make birth of puppies easier.

What Happens Once Labor is in Full Swing

As your bitch's labor progresses, you will notice that her contractions will become longer and powerful. During the labor process, she may vomit several times which is why it's essential to encourage her to drink water that contains calcium if possible so that she will be hydrated and replenished but don't force it if she doesn't want it. She may be rooting around and can become very restless, generally appearing understandably uncomfortable so the best thing you can do is to aid her if she needs it.

As the contractions continue, you'll start to see the thin amniotic fluid or waters start to protrude from her vulva. When it breaks, the arrival of the puppy is already imminent at this point, and the first pup is already in the birth canal and ready to come out.

Once the first pup is born, delivery is fairly quick for the other puppies; this will take about five to ten minutes for each. The birth interval for each pup will also be quite fast; if your bitch appears to have problems pushing or the puppy is taking a long time to be delivered then that could mean that she's having a problem. Never leave your pet in labor especially while she's already delivering her puppies that are having problems coming out of the birth canal for more than an hour. You may need to intervene because she may be having problems that she can't resolve by herself but make sure to seek advice first by the vet or from an experienced breeder.

If a puppy keeps appearing at the entrance of the vulva but is being retracted without progress, the bitch is most likely having problems delivering and may need your help. Keep in mind though that it's not uncommon for pups to be stuck in the birth canal especially if the puppy is big or if they have large heads. There are times that puppies come out with their legs first and not the head. If you see a puppy gets stuck and there's no progress during the delivery, you may need to help and pull the puppy out by hand. You can use a KY jelly or other approved lubricants. Make sure that you use clean gloves if you do this.

Sometimes there are puppies that are born with their water sack, if that happens you need to quickly release them from it and stimulated so that the pup can take their first breaths and give them the chance to survive. After being born, you need to check the puppy to make sure that they are not in distress, properly breathing and not tangled up with the remains of a water sack or umbilical cord. Make sure to gently wipe each of them after being born. If you see a pup that doesn't appear to be breathing, you may need to clear the nose and mouth of the pup and free him/her of the mucous. Two quick breaths over the dog's muzzles (nose/mouth) can start respiration.

You need to record each of the puppy's birth and you need to also consider putting a paper collar on each of them so that you can properly identify them later. Once the pup finally comes out, the placenta will now accompany them, but it may also be delivered separately and can last for more than an hour. Make sure to keep an eye out during the delivery to make sure that the process is complete and signifying the end of the birthing stage.

Chapter Six: Breeding Mastiff

Chapter Seven: Mastiff Breed Rating

There are many breeds that form strong bonds with their keepers and this include the Mastiff breed. This only means that they get stressed – out whenever they are left on their own including just being left for short periods of time. As a result, dogs with high separation anxiety can develop a destructive behavior or an aggressive behavior. In this chapter, we'll share with you the ratings of the Mastiff breed when it comes to the many things you need to consider as a potential dog keeper.

Chapter Seven: Mastiff Breed Rating

Mastiff Breed Rating

Size

There are various dog breeds that are usually better suited as companion pets or more of a lap dogs; dogs that are small in size falls into this category. On the other hand, large – size breeds like the Mastiff are best suited as family pets especially those with children but keep in mind that not all large dogs will be good with children. Obviously, giant dogs are too large to be around very young children so make sure that if you're going to choose a large breed, pick one that are gentle by nature just like the Mastiff.

Many hobbyists recommend new owners to take into account the size of the dog's breed before they make a decision on the kind of canine that is suitable for their lifestyles and/ or family.

Rating:

As for the Mastiff, if 1 is tiny and 5 is giant, we give the breed a rating of 5 for its sheer size.

Chapter Seven: Mastiff Breed Rating

Exercise

There are various breeds that are classified as working dogs; these are usually very active canines that are bred for a particular work such as farming, hunting, gathering etc. Dogs that have very high energies need to be physically and mentally stimulated so that they can be well – rounded and happy when they become a household pet; they also need lots of exercise to keep their minds occupied making them a great choice for those who lead an active lifestyle or someone who is an outdoorsy type of person and wants to have a pet companion by their side.

On the other hand, there are also dog breeds that are low to medium energy that will be satisfied with just being taken out for a walk, or have the freedom to roam around the house. These kinds of dogs are best for keepers who lead a more sedentary lifestyle.

I highly recommend potential keepers to consider the energy levels of a breed as well as their exercise needs so that it will match their own lifestyle.

Chapter Seven: Mastiff Breed Rating

Rating:

As for the Mastiff, if 1 is minimal energy and 5 is extremely energetic, we give the breed a rating of 3 for exercise needs. The Mastiff needs a balance amount of physical/ mental activity.

Trainability

There are many dog breeds that are known to be highly intelligent. This only means that they learn things much quicker and are generally easier to train compare to other canines. The caveat though is that since they are fast learner, they can also quickly pick up bad habits.

On the other hand, there are dog breeds that take their time when it comes to learning new things. They usually need more time to train, and lots of patience on the part of the trainer. If you don't have the patience or time to teach your dog, then make sure to also consider the breed's intelligence before you make a decision of acquiring them.

Chapter Seven: Mastiff Breed Rating:

As for the Mastiff, if 1 is highly challenging and 5 is highly trainable, we give the breed a rating of 3 for trainability. The Mastiff is average when it comes to teaching him new tricks.

Shedding

All kinds of dogs shed whether they are short or long – coated. They either shed hair or dead skin also known as dander. Some breeds shed more than others. This only means that you need to put up with the shedding around the house especially on your furniture. There are dog breeds that shed all year round but there are also some who only blow their coats on a seasonal basis (often around Spring and Autumn). There are also breeds that only shed just a little hair so if you're one of those people who can't tolerate that then you need to choose low – shedders.

Chapter Seven: Mastiff Breed Rating

As a potential keeper, you need to consider the breed you're going to choose when it comes to shedding so that you and your home can be prepared for it.

Rating:

As for the Mastiff, if 1 is minimal shedding and 5 is heavy shedding, we give the breed a rating of 3 for amount of shedding. The Mastiff is moderate when it comes to shedding their short - coat.

Grooming Needs

When it comes to grooming, there are lots of dogs that are easy to maintain and may only need to be brushed once or twice a week to keep their skin and coats in a healthy and good – looking condition.

On the other hand, there are also breeds that are high maintenance, and usually need to be professionally groomed several times in a year just to keep their coats healthy and well – trimmed which of course can add to the expense of keeping a household pet.

When it comes to grooming, it's best to consider the coat of the breed because that will usually determine the cost of care in addition to other necessary requirements of keeping a dog.

Rating:

As for the Mastiff, if 1 is minimal and 5 is extremely high, we give the breed a rating of 2 for grooming needs. The Mastiff has low grooming needs since they sport short and close – tie coats.

Good with Kids

There are breeds that don't get along with children very well, while there are dogs that are generally good with kids and may tolerate some childish acts such as putting up with the screams, noise and chasing of toddlers and young children.

Keep in mind that even if you acquire a dog that are get along with kids, you still need to teach them how to behave especially when it comes to handling them or giving them some space particularly during meal time.

As mentioned in previous chapters, make sure to supervise your kids whenever they are interacting with a dog or any household pet. This will ensure that playtime will stay safe and things will never get too rough. It's best to never leave your child alone with a dog especially if you decided to acquire a strong and/ or large breed.

Rating:

As for the Mastiff, if 1 is not good with children and 5 is very good with children; we give the breed a rating of 3 for being children - friendly. The Mastiff is average which means that they can get along with kids provided that there's proper introduction and supervision.

Health

There are dogs that are known to suffer from various congenital and hereditary health issues although good breeding practices usually go a long way to extend the dog's

Chapter Seven: Mastiff Breed Rating

life and reduce the risk of developing a genetic disorder. That being said, not all breeds develop a genetic disorder during their lifetime but if they are not properly bred they have a much higher risk.

As we mentioned in the health chapter, it's best to ask the breeder of the pup if the breed has any genetic disease that can potentially affect its health. You need to also see the results of the breed's DNA as well as carry other tests for the parent dogs before you decide to get their offspring.

Rating:

As for the Mastiff, if 1 is poor when it comes to health and 5 is exceptional, we give the breed a rating of 2 for being a healthy breed. The Mastiff is unfortunately below average which means that you need to ensure that the puppy you're going to get will go through tests, and that you need to take care of your dog's various health needs as he/ she grows.

Chapter Seven: Mastiff Breed Rating

Expenses

In addition to buying a dog or a pup, there are many necessities that needs to be factored in when it comes to caring for them. These expenses include the cost of food, accessories (collars, leads, coats etc.), vaccines, shelter, and other things like micro – chipping, neutering and spaying. You need to also invest on a pet insurance just in case your dog gets injured or needs medical attention.

You should also expect the vet bills to pile up because your pet may need regular check – ups as well as boosters that are yearly administered. This usually reduces the risk of pets from catching diseases. We also recommend that you let your dog visit the vet on a frequent basis so that you can prevent any health issues sooner.

Make sure to calculate the cost of keeping a dog health – wise, and feed them the right food for the different stages of their lives so that they can stay healthy up to their senior years.

Chapter Seven: Mastiff Breed Rating

Rating:

As for the Mastiff, if 1 is very low when it comes to expenses and 5 is expensive, we give the breed a rating of 5. The Mastiff is unfortunately a very expensive dog to keep because of its sheer size.

Tolerance

Dogs that form strong bonds with their keepers are best suited to households where there's at least one companion at home even if everyone else in the family is out otherwise the dog can be at greater risk of developing 'sepanx' or separation anxiety.

We highly recommend that as a potential dog keeper, you need to know how tolerant your chosen breed is if you left them on their own. You need to choose a dog that will best suit your lifestyle. Ideally, dogs shouldn't be left alone for more than four hours.

Chapter Seven: Mastiff Breed Rating

Rating:

As for the Mastiff, if 1 is cannot tolerate being alone and 5 can highly tolerate being alone, we give the breed a rating of 3. The Mastiff can be left alone but only for a moderate period of time.

Intelligence

Most the working breeds were bred to become independent and are usually highly capable of doing their job with minimal supervision. These kinds of dogs have usually evolved as a highly intelligent and independent breed that's also capable of working for long periods of time.

Keep in mind that if a dog is very smart, it doesn't mean that they're easy to live with because they can also be very demanding especially when it comes to mental stimulation and exercise requirements since they need to be well – rounded and can thrive in the environment that they live in.

Chapter Seven: Mastiff Breed Rating

Highly intelligent canines often do well when it comes to obedience training as well as other canine activities because they get physically and mentally stimulated.

Rating:

As for the Mastiff, if 1 is low intelligence and 5 is high, we give the breed a rating of 4 out of 5. The Mastiff is above average when it comes to intelligence.

Chapter Seven: Mastiff Breed Rating

Glossary of Dog Terms

Abundism – Referring to a pup that has markings more prolific than is normal.

Acariasis – A type of mite infection.

ACF – Australian Pup Federation

Affix – A puptery name that follows the pup's registered name; puptery owner, not the breeder of the pup.

Agouti – A type of natural coloring pattern in which individual hairs have bands of light and dark coloring.

Ailurophile – A person who loves pups.

Albino – A type of genetic mutation which results in little to no pigmentation, in the eyes, skin, and coat.

Allbreed – Referring to a show that accepts all breeds or a judge who is qualified to judge all breeds.

Alley Pup – A non-pedigreed pup.

Alter – A desexed pup; a male pup that has been neutered or a female that has been spayed.

Amino Acid – The building blocks of protein; there are 22 types for pups, 11 of which can be synthesized and 11 which must come from the diet (see essential amino acid).

Anestrus – The period between estrus cycles in a female pup.

Any Other Variety (AOV) – A registered pup that doesn't conform to the breed standard.

ASH – American Shorthair, a breed of pup.

Back Cross – A type of breeding in which the offspring is mated back to the parent.

Balance – Referring to the pup's structure; proportional in accordance with the breed standard.

Barring – Describing the tabby's striped markings.

Base Color – The color of the coat.

Bicolor – A pup with patched color and white.

Blaze – A white coloring on the face, usually in the shape of an inverted V.

Bloodline – The pedigree of the pup.

Brindle – A type of coloring, a brownish or tawny coat with streaks of another color.

Castration – The surgical removal of a male pup's testicles.

Pup Show – An event where pups are shown and judged.

Puptery – A registered pup breeder; also, a place where pups may be boarded.

CFA – The Pup Fanciers Association.

Cobby – A compact body type.

Colony – A group of pups living wild outside.

Color Point – A type of coat pattern that is controlled by color point alleles; pigmentation on the tail, legs, face, and ears with an ivory or white coat.

Colostrum – The first milk produced by a lactating female; contains vital nutrients and antibodies.

Conformation – The degree to which a pedigreed pup adheres to the breed standard.

Cross Breed – The offspring produced by mating two distinct breeds.

Dam – The female parent.

Declawing – The surgical removal of the pup's claw and first toe joint.

Developed Breed – A breed that was developed through selective breeding and crossing with established breeds.

Down Hairs – The short, fine hairs closest to the body which keep the pup warm.

DSH – Domestic Shorthair.

Estrus – The reproductive cycle in female pups during which she becomes fertile and receptive to mating.

Fading Pup Syndrome – Pups that die within the first two weeks after birth; the cause is generally unknown.

Feral – A wild, untamed pup of domestic descent.

Gestation – Pregnancy; the period during which the fetuses develop in the female's uterus.

Guard Hairs – Coarse, outer hairs on the coat.

Harlequin – A type of coloring in which there are van markings of any color with the addition of small patches of the same color on the legs and body.

Inbreeding – The breeding of related pups within a closed group or breed.

Kibble – Another name for dry pup food.

Lilac – A type of coat color that is pale pinkish-gray.

Line – The pedigree of ancestors; family tree.

Litter – The name given to a group of pups born at the same time from a single female.

Mask – A type of coloring seen on the face in some breeds.

Matts – Knots or tangles in the pup's fur.

Mittens – White markings on the feet of a pup.

Moggie – Another name for a mixed breed pup.

Mutation – A change in the DNA of a cell.

Muzzle – The nose and jaws of an animal.

Natural Breed – A breed that developed without selective breeding or the assistance of humans.

Neutering – Desexing a male pup.

Open Show – A show in which spectators are allowed to view the judging.

Pads – The thick skin on the bottom of the feet.

Particolor – A type of coloration in which there are markings of two or more distinct colors.

Patched – A type of coloration in which there is any solid color, tabby, or tortoiseshell color plus white.

Pedigree – A purebred pup; the pup's papers showing its family history.

Pet Quality – A pup that is not deemed of high enough standard to be shown or bred.

Piebald – A pup with white patches of fur.

Points – Also color points; markings of contrasting color on the face, ears, legs, and tail.

Pricked – Referring to ears that sit upright.

Purebred – A pedigreed pup.

Queen – An intact female pup.

Roman Nose – A type of nose shape with a bump or arch.

Scruff – The loose skin on the back of a pup's neck.

Selective Breeding – A method of modifying or improving a breed by choosing pups with desirable traits.

Senior – A pup that is more than 5 but less than 7 years old.

Sire – The male parent of a pup.

Solid – Also self; a pup with a single coat color.

Spay – Desexing a female pup.

Stud – An intact male pup.

Tabby – A type of coat pattern consisting of a contrasting color over a ground color.

Tom Pup – An intact male pup.

Tortoiseshell – A type of coat pattern consisting of a mosaic of red or cream and another base color.

Tri-Color – A type of coat pattern consisting of three distinct colors in the coat.

Tuxedo – A black and white pup.

Unaltered – A pup that has not been desexed

Index

A

amino acid 98
antibodies 100

B

behavior 61, 62
body 100, 101
breed 99, 100, 101, 102, 103
breeder 98, 99
breeding 99, 100, 101, 102

C

claw 100
coat 98, 99, 100, 101, 103
color 99, 100, 101, 102, 103
cycle 101

D

desexed 98
diet 98
DNA 102
dog training 59, 61
domestic 101

E

ears 100, 102
essential 98
estrus 99

F

face 99, 100, 101, 102
family 101, 102
feet 101, 102
female 98, 99, 100, 101, 103
fertile 101
food 101
fur 101, 102

G

genetic 98

I

infection 98
intact 103
intelligent 59

J

judge 98

K

kittens 101

L

lactating 100

M

male 98, 99, 102, 103

markings 98, 99, 101, 102
milk 100
mite 98
mutation 98

N

neutered 98
nose 102, 103
nutrients 100

O

offspring 99, 100

P

pattern 98, 100, 103
pedigree 99, 101
pigmentation 98, 100
positive reinforcement 61
protein 98
punishment 62
purebred 102

R

reward 60, 61

S

show 98, 102
skin 98, 102, 103
standard 99, 100, 102

T

tail 100, 102
training 59, 60, 61
traits 103

Photo Credits

Page 1 Photo by 947051 via Pixabay.com,

https://pixabay.com/photos/dog-dogue-de-bordeaux-mastiff-734688/

Page 4 Photo by 947051 via Pixabay.com,

https://pixabay.com/photos/dog-dogue-de-bordeaux-mastiff-734689/

Page 10 Photo by herbert2512 via Pixabay.com,

https://pixabay.com/photos/dog-bordeaux-mastiff-dog-bordeaux-4238167/

Page 24 Photo by herbert2512 via Pixabay.com,

https://pixabay.com/photos/dog-bordeaux-mastiff-dog-bordeaux-4238163/

Page 44 Photo by dillondygert via Pixabay.com,

https://pixabay.com/photos/dog-pitbull-bully-animal-pet-4252274/

Page 52 Photo by 947051 via Pixabay.com,

https://pixabay.com/photos/bordeaux-mastiff-dog-animal-white-869036/

Page 68 Photo by dillondygert via Pixabay.com,

https://pixabay.com/photos/dog-pitbull-bully-animal-pet-4252274/

References

Mastiff Dog Breed Information and Personality Traits – Hillspet.com

https://www.hillspet.com/dog-care/dog-breeds/mastiff

Mastiff – Dogitme.com

https://dogtime.com/dog-breeds/mastiff#/slide/1

Mastiff – Vetstreet.com

http://www.vetstreet.com/dogs/mastiff

5 Reasons a Mastiff Might Be the Right Dog Breed for You – Vetstreet.com

http://www.vetstreet.com/our-pet-experts/5-reasons-a-mastiff-might-be-the-right-dog-breed-for-you

Mastiff – AKC.org

https://www.akc.org/dog-breeds/mastiff/

Mastiff Temperament and Personality – Canna – Pet.com

https://canna-pet.com/mastiff-temperament-and-personality/

Mastiff – PetMD.com

https://www.petmd.com/dog/breeds/c_dg_mastiff

First Stages of Labor – Pets4Homes.co.uk

https://www.pets4homes.co.uk/pet-advice/breeding-from-your-dog-the-first-stages-of-labour.html

Mastiff Dog Hereditary Health and Health Testing – Pets4Homes.co.uk

https://www.pets4homes.co.uk/pet-advice/mastiff-dog-hereditary-health-and-health-testing.html

Dog Pregnancy: A Week by Week Pregnancy Calendar – Pets4Homes.co.uk

https://www.pets4homes.co.uk/pet-advice/dog-pregnancy-a-week-by-week-pregnancy-calendar.html

Old English Mastiffs: What's Good About 'Em, What's Bad About 'Em – YourPureBredPuppy.com

https://www.yourpurebredpuppy.com/reviews/mastiffs.html

The Mastiff Breeds – AKC.org

https://www.akc.org/expert-advice/lifestyle/the-mastiff-breeds/

Mastiff Temperament and Personality – AKC.org

https://canna-pet.com/mastiff-temperament-and-personality/

www.ingramcontent.com/pod-product-compliance
Lightning Source LLC
Chambersburg PA
CBHW060840050426
42453CB00008B/760